COSMOS

COSMOS

A POEM

JAMES APPLEWHITE

 Louisiana State University Press
Baton Rouge

Publication of this book is made possible in part by support from Duke University.

Published by Louisiana State University Press
Copyright © 2014 by James Applewhite
All rights reserved
Manufactured in the United States of America
LSU Press Paperback Original
First printing

Designer: Laura Roubique Gleason
Typeface: Calluna

Library of Congress Cataloging-in-Publication Data
Applewhite, James.
 [Poems. Selections]
 Cosmos : A Poem / James Applewhite.
    pages cm
 "LSU Press Paperback Original."
 ISBN 978-0-8071-5499-1 (paper : alk. paper) — ISBN 978-0-8071-5501-1 (epub) — ISBN 978-0-8071-5500-4 (pdf) — ISBN 978-0-8071-5502-8 (mobi)
 I. Title.
 PS3551.P67A6 2014
 811'.54—dc23

2013021066

Grateful acknowledgment is made to the editors of the following publications, in which the poems listed first appeared: *Georgia Review:* "Reforested Land"; *Hampden-Sydney Poetry Review:* "First Star" (as "Star on the River"); *Hudson Review:* "The Late April Garden"; *Maulana Azad Journal of the English Language and Literature (MAJELL):* "The Home Place"; *North Carolina Literary Review:* "Unpublished Interview," "Repairing the Farmhouse," "Driving from Columbia," "A Hotel Tower above Oahu," "Reading the Science News"; *Pembroke Magazine:* "The Language of Space and Time" (as "The Language of Space"); *27 Views of Durham:* "In the Gardens beside a Library."

The paper in this book meets the guidelines for permanence and durability of the Committee on Production Guidelines for Book Longevity of the Council on Library Resources. ∞

CONTENTS

Reading the Science News   1
A Premonition   2
Night Writing   3
The Guests   5
Platonic Astronomy   6
Cooper's Hawk   7
Two in October Light   9
Practice Bombing   10
The Sea Connection   11
A Cemetery in Normandy   12
In the Gardens beside a Library   14
Anthropic Cosmological Principle   15
Hemlock Hill   17
Learning the Directions   19
Unpublished Interview   23
Repairing the Farmhouse   25
The Home Place   27
Reforested Land   29
A Hotel Tower above Oahu   30
The Late April Garden   31
Conversation in Faculty Commons   33
First Light   50
The Shadowed Counterpane   51
Imagining Origin   52
Time in the First Village   56
Membrane Theory   58
Quest for Beginning   59
First Star   60
Coming Home in the Dark   62
The Language of Space and Time   64
Driving from Columbia   66

COSMOS

READING THE SCIENCE NEWS

New York Times, *July 2010*

"We've known for a long time gravity
doesn't exist," Dr. Verlinde said.
This adhesion of all mass to itself is
following the vector of energy downward
with the thermodynamic arrow, which pierces us
with our moments. The illusion encloses,
scenes in mind return nonsensically—
my foot slips on the slick bank and for
a moment suspended in falling
I know the time slow down, seeing
the red-star sweet gum leaf
sliding with the current's surface
that holds the late September sky
and heat in a thin film.

Then I pierce it, splashing through—
the rowboat my brother called the Peanut Shell
rocking out from the bank while
I arise back through the brown creek
skin and into air of the dream world
I know so well, where Henry is laughing.

I see a long-legged water strider
dimpling the tension.
The water strider and I stay fixed in motion
while I swim for the Peanut Shell
and flop and rock my way inside
where I am still, in the dimension
of that separate day, the boat
drifting not to anywhere but here,
the red, five-pointed leaf afloat beside.

A PREMONITION

The rain comes almost silently,
a gift from the sky to the grass and forest.
The big leaves of the fig bush tip and dip,
the dogwood branches elastically vibrate,
the crape myrtle feels its bloom-crown moved
like a mind accepting beauty from starlight.
Wind stirs the oaks the maples the tulip poplar,
the glistening, new-leaved beech,
in quietly ecstatic celebration. All
trees and bushes and lowly grasses
endure their mute, uncommunicable
connection into life of the subsoil
for moments like these.
Even if the uniformed caretakers of parks
and forests lose sight of their glory,
these green, long-lived beings, rooted
for life in their one place, possess it.
In this first coming of the rain
a simple sacred communion,
at the edge of perception,
murmurs from one to another.

NIGHT WRITING

Tonight again it spins
its lines on the air
suspends its triangle there
from a camellia sasanqua

to the white crape myrtle
to a corner of the portico.
Aloof from my wonder
patiently swiftly it inscribes

its radials then overlays
circles, touching loosening
trailing a shining
between the lit house and riverward darkness.

A dog barks from over
the river. Wild or domestic?
I don't care. I like to hear
sounds measure the distance.

Among wide stirrings in trees
the crystalline webbing flexes.
Each line sways and stays
shining its way toward a nexus

each thought an instant's design
a pane inscribed on the wind.
I drift in toward bedtime.
These connections remind

me of sleep when filaments
of likeness blow in by chance—
houses adrift on darkness
faces that loved me once.

THE GUESTS

The long-legged late summer fawn
flicks its lanceolate, rose-veined ears,
nipping at yellow jackets circling our birdbath.
Its almond eyes and black nose compose
an alert serenity. What has it to fear?
It finishes the last of a red begonia, then,
upon the higher, rock-walled terrace, nibbles
a cotoneaster—planted decades ago by
our son, who, between his college years,
worked for a nursery. Such park creatures,
since our grownup children's departures,
move more comfortably in—so distantly kin,
that we regard each other in an interested
silence. Well, our second family.
But I can't speak to them, except on
this paper, that only our own kind see.
Growing older is also gradually lonelier.
The other fawn retains his infant spotting,
is smaller, shyer, and nibbles now
peacefully, caged within azalea stems.
We will visit our elder son this weekend—
and grandson Christian, who once learned
to collect deer bones with me, searching along
a ridge beside the river, behind our dwelling.
We live here still, among the many stars
that gather over our final precious evenings.

PLATONIC ASTRONOMY

I focus the home-built refractor. Thought
concentrates, its angle infinitely acute
the energy-density absolute.
Mind aches with the radiant
hope that sharpens toward a star
lending sequence to this *before,*
as if all time had come from this pure
precedent. And now I have it,
Vega's blue-white dot
trembling in the eyepiece
like a flake of space ice.
These lenses focus the beam,
collapsing a crossing of time
into this instant.

I feel mind and sky correspond.
An inner light turned
outward that I fleetingly catch
lets mind and image match.
I think of space compressed to a point
the star in my eyepiece like sex
the idea like physical climax.

Sight of it dawns like a music.
The beauty of light its slight weight
moving through as the material moment
of thought measures a distance
from the origin point
into the grace of existence.

COOPER'S HAWK

On the lid of our garbage cart
it plucked the breast feathers out
having eaten the head for a start.

It now turned the breast meat back
and stretched gut-strings with its beak.
Sharp-clawed and sleek

it tore the dead thrush apart, pulling
the flight feathers out, disassembling
the one it had bested, swooping and killing—

or, I thought, perhaps cleaning the carcass
for nestlings, offspring its success.
But I saw it keep on eating, the mess

of fluff around them both what was left
of the call of the thrush, one also best
when hunting and pouncing, among our massed

azaleas. Brown-winged as the leaves it just
now had hopped among, its breast
was white-dappled rust, all singing past.

Then the Cooper's started at a whir:
a bicyclist down the hill, predator-
like to the hawk, so quick in departure

my binocular's field couldn't follow.
Disappearing like a vision, so hollow
of beak and eye, it figured no sorrow

for the thrush, whose rich meat it took.
It left me feathers, bits of flesh, the look
at a survival-selector, its beak a hook.

TWO IN OCTOBER LIGHT

for Jan

Unbelievably the Earth rotates on
its axis so that the color of light
turns precious in altering, a rich

umber already on the dogwood leaf
where beauty in mortality burns
darkly this afternoon. The spectrum

says that its colors mean union
in a white as permanent as we imagine—
a warmth on the hand a reddening

on the ripe fig high up in the bush
that I pick at your loving request
for our salad this evening. Touching

the back of my hand the sunbeam
illuminates a map of my years, a record
of veins, scars, purple discolorations.

My soul knows itself by this tinct
of beauty that my body feels as the intent
of my mind to understand softens

and the coming ending of maroon and golden
colors the instinct for light with mercy
as I discover the truth of the one flesh

in gratefulness for your sole companionship,
this love you evoke for you as myself
this time of union that justifies suffering.

PRACTICE BOMBING

Emerald Isle, N.C.

At first inside the beach house
I think it is a giant scraping
of timbers together—but construction—
at night? Then outside I see flashings
on the horizon, brightenings as with
lightning but the stars shine clear.
Then airborne motors rumble their blades,
they beat distant winds where something
is crumpling the air, smashings as of
homes collapsing like cardboard boxes
underfoot of Paul Bunyan and his ox.
But machines and their men are bombing
the far river. I remember, we were told.
Blasts flare tissue-soft over the pine trees,
as the lag of concussions places safety
within the many miles between us.
This is my country practicing destruction.
The old couple who watched from their Ford
from the last century as the real estate
agent departed are too late to sell
their almost seaside cottage for a fortune.
Cassiopeia is spangling its splayed W
toward the pole, the Pleiades shine on
like a swarm of golden bees, Hercules
and Pegasus have rarely heard such fuss
from our invisible planet since Fat Man
and Little Boy incinerated two cities.
O Vega pierce us with your blue beam
arrow, O Orion lay down our swords.
They burn on, blue and white—or reddish,
Mars-like, iron-making giants, inconstant
as we are, inheritors of heavenly war—
of self-sacrifice to the violent constellations.

THE SEA CONNECTION

Ripples in the sand correspond
to waves in the sound, in the wind.
I feel the rough-leaved cinquefoils
holding me, though my mind
soars out with the wind-slanting tern
aching to discover the old connection.
The fishermen with their rods like antennas
are catching slight signals, the mullets
and trouts they pull in hold omens in guts.
The sea oat stems stand seed-hung
from long times of accepting the sea wind
curving with it from the breakers inland,
roots holding sand against the ocean.
Along this line of union, they sift down
the blown grains, netting underground,
arising along the slopes they have made, in shapes
like the whale backs as large as dunes
far out, that few living here have seen—
bodies emerging from the body of ocean
spouting spume in their surfacing
breathing as they learned when inland.

A CEMETERY IN NORMANDY

Morning glories twine rough burdocks,
blackberries like wild roses
white-bloom in salt air, where
an army came in from the sea.

Ignorant of the formality erecting
the Norman spires on inland,
they came, unpacked on the beach
from Higgins boats, to face

the German eighty-eights: precise,
sighted-in, from concrete domes
set in this fertile soil
like minds gone mad with iron.

The present tide inscribes
its pools and cursive runnels—
a giant hieroglyphic, illegible,
to us, among these craters and fragments.

Only swallows, hovering in sea wind,
seem to understand, cherishing
their moment on wing,
above this living coast

where many men lost life.
They suggest this fragrance as joy—
a hay tinge in sea air, where
shells hurtled, where now the rosy burdocks

bend their heraldic heads to breezes—
where a mint scent of grasses
wafts to us the coast's surviving sentience.
We accept their sacrifice as a grace—

an unintended atonement—
and read our freedom
between the moving sea
and rows of stones just inland.

IN THE GARDENS BESIDE A LIBRARY

The willow oak has written in it
an ink of time-underlayment.
I say the word *emeritus*
and the wind-rubbed coppery surface
touches my eyes like a worn rug.
Corded by limbs to a base in soil
it recovers those years of toil
that layered other leaves in another place.
The library's vellum and coffee still drug
my memory, like Gothic walls and trees above.
There I and my gnarled masters strove,
limning interpretive cursives and dots
onto the passionate dead's still living arguments.

There wide-browed Lionel carried his satchel
into the crenellated tower, kindly, impersonal
and shone his lamp through a diamonded
window, out toward me, where I read
my fortune through the screening tree
and fed ideals on its shadowy history.

The fortress-like place of these pasts,
standing behind me, casts
no shade on my course
where free in the twilight I pass
the labeled species, these knowledge-trees—
not reading, and with no remorse.

As I walk farther on
one orange-green golden
final maple says that vision
is wisdom, that beauty is changing
and is its own meaning.
This space of time is at last my own.

ANTHROPIC COSMOLOGICAL PRINCIPLE

> If true, it is somehow magic.... we are here, because we have been lucky, because for this particular universe the lottery produced a certain set of numbers, which allow the universe to have an evolution, which is very long.
> —Guido Tonelli, CERN, *New York Times,* March 5, 2013

So we bead the skein of time
in a cosmos orderly and random
free among determinants
breeding descendants
riding the one-way arrow
uncanny to us consciously.
We know only the autumn parkway
suspended by a granite mountain
below beech and maple yellows
among iron-rust oaks like the armor
of dead Vikings—the panorama receding
in stilled waves of Earth-crust folding
leaving the motion only evening
felt coming in the turning
of the monolith mountain.

Spruces spike up, bronze-evergreen
among earthward deciduous longings
as a radiance strikes us
from a hawk-winged point in the distance.

Bedazzled by the chance of consciousness
our breathing inconstantly praises
these decrees of the stars.
Our years have followed
the curve of horizon at evening
marking arcs within it of

our infants' buttocks and cheeks
our tears and fingernail moons,
accepting this good luck of time
within an autumn wind leaving
the taste of color in mind—
a chill still young
upon our faces and the flavor
of the body of a co-life lover
on the tongue.

HEMLOCK HILL

Banner Elk, N.C.

Up Hemlock Hill, petrified-looking hemlocks
wind their ashen branches among beeches and oaks,
the feathery ghost-crowns arising as if smokes
from dead fires. One marbled trunk reminds
me of an abandoned column—of when grinds
of folding basalt, gneiss and conglomerate
echoed in an earlier world, would incorporate
this quartz vein bright at my feet.

From lower, where the forest returns,
I see the hemlocks' branches stream westward,
weathervanes frozen in a cosmic wind
that I seem walking into, here by the pond.
Young mallards paddle the surface
while elders drop feathers and waste on grass.

The weather changes, low clouds pass
and trail gray mist and bits of ice.
I face a rushing, gusting turbulence
that piles up waves along the water's course.

Yet Elk River runs crystalline
though this surface roughness seems feeding ruin.
I see the real current flow underneath,
and align myself with this counterforce
that shaped first chaos, in igniting birth
of the stars—one star the sun of our Earth.

I walk and ponder until it is late,
seeing beech branches fine against twilight.
Then mallards vee down from last flights,
alighting a darkening lake for the night.
As elders and their ducklings turn

toward shore, their wakes intertwine,
these intersecting circles and straights
an interface of motion and stasis—
my always-illusion, in mountain darkness.

LEARNING THE DIRECTIONS

That small world where my soul was inserted
fell from a hill crest south, toward low-lying
fields which the river flooded. The slick-roiled pulsing
siphoned away time below the bridge, through
the fisherman's moccasin-haunted banks, where
a plank-built boat rode chained on the nudging current.
I climbed from its overflow, awakening.

Houses stood along that riverward slant,
where I felt people's lives in the cells of rooms.
Soon, I crossed between our two-story house and
that of my grandparents. My mind mapped out where
Grandfather's garden and chicken yard lay, past
the scuppernong's swelling, pillowy tangle
over the six-foot wooden fence. There I remembered
how, inside his packhouse, air felt greasy with
the hams and shoulders that had touched my cheeks.

Then I passed the clinic where Dr. Darden had sat,
fat in his castered chair, before a roll-top desk,
freezing my ringworm with his silver sprayer.
Alongside, a street led away into the brightness
of the fields—a concave of sky over corn, where sun
ignited the invisible air, at a height to behold
a world below, from a steep intensity of heat.

I saw, deep in the Coleys' porch, the daybed where
Miss Ada Gray had reclined to recover—it pensive
still, before the too-tall curtained windows. She had rested,
prone with T.B.—a shivery word for a child,
sound-reminding of *sanitorium,* and Wilson.
But that was west and north, past the ridged-up
railroad tracks that divided the village's houses

and churches and market and stores from the dangerous
wail of the sawmill. Its shark-toothed shining circle
ripped up the pine logs that smelled like Christmas.

My father's service station lay also across
the tracks—where the steam locomotive had whooshed
in passing, hissing with vacuum brakes, smelling
of a metal world. Over these steel, parallel lines,
polished by the linked wheels, the water tank tower
stood giantly silver, its flashing height like
a Martian fighting machine. The sun-gleam
crowned its conical hat with a killing brilliance.
The horror of hurtling bodies of silver and olive drab,
diving and bombing, in radio static, and flickering
in movie newsreels, swirled still in air, around
these great Martian legs, that suspended the tank
like the Tallboy bomb I'd read of. It seemed
continually to be falling, when I looked straight up:
sighted-in by crosshairs, exactly where Main Street
intersected the railroad. There, trains hauled change
on past us, the long flatcars hurtling along at dusk,
bearing khaki trucks with white stars on doors,
the tanks with their molded-steel, menacingly
rounded, hard-headed turrets and projecting guns
jolting on quickly before me and my father,
our breath sucked out by that war-velocity,
while I felt his blunt wounded fingers that kept
him to fight on the home front. The plate glass
behind us showed the discredited peacetime furniture,
the sofas for families to loll on, lazily together.

Now war-fear blew through like a black wind,
sending my father back to his station after supper for
a last lonely patrol, in front of his gas pumps—

the Esso-ovals like military insignia upon them.
The bulbs around his shelter extended their light,
above piled tires, in a perimeter holding back darkness.
Those summers, multitudes of moths had
circled the bulbs, casting their magnified shadows,
flickering out onto the chinaberry trees and
cabins where the cooks and sawmill workers
of a darker color lived—where sometimes I
had played, with the fragrant, comfortable-
feeling kids, in their game-marked sandy clay.
Then, with my rheumatic fever, a woe led east,
and frighteningly through the sun-down fields,
past barns and over bridges, of those places
I'd never seen at evening, to the children's
hospital at Greenville. Its rectangle of halls,
and needles afterward, towered in dreams, far beyond
its six-story height in daylight. The cots of our ward
reminded me of newsreel orphans in Poland.
The inky tentacles, that the octopus-Axis reached
out in *Life* magazine, had touched us likewise.
My father was home but absent, Mother's fear
for my too-quick heart sending needles of chill
through the yellow-lighted circle over suppers.
Later, he carried me in his arms and ascended
the perilous wooden stairs to the roof of his shelter,
which the Civilian Spotter's Station commanded.
There he showed me the official handbook,
thick like my Boy Scout manual but crowded
with silhouettes of warplanes, below photos
and data of performance and armaments.

The dark-angel Luftwaffe noses, blunted by
cannons, the wing-tips clipped like their crosses,
revealed evil against good. The heroine Spitfire

defended the Wesley-homeland of Mother's dreams,
turning its elliptical wings in circles
tighter than its foes'. Leather-clad fliers
flared man-woeful in baleful wail
and fell—their beards glowing with an iron yelling
I heard in mind, mouthed by male devils
still human, whose wreckage I burned with.

I died as the one I was, arising *other*,
a quick pulse changing my time to fever.
All I was ever to know, I learned—
willing within my mind, dreaming against dying.

UNPUBLISHED INTERVIEW

Seymour Johnson Air Force Base, 1980

On an airfield carved from farms,
the olive domes held bombs.
These nuclear igloos—houses for gnomes,
in a grim fairy tale—were why I had come.
On runways, the B-52's stood hulking, gross,
not as seen aloft: swept-wing cathedrals,
nacelles horizontally aspiring, flying
buttresses of lift supporting a nave of aluminum,
the narthex cockpit, clerestory turrets. Angels
of death over Vietnam jungles,
they had pressed their stress into my sanctum
of memory, reanimating the heightened dying
I'd dreamed, during childhood war. Up close,
they loomed oddly real and unreal, small and vast—
facts I'd imagined, stationarily fast.
The flyers talked of their training as an ordinary job:
this following of the chart toward a "drop,"
where coordinates crossed. I couldn't imagine
Wilson or Rocky Mount or Greensboro a focus
of this grown-up play—this oblivion-practice.
"But that's the way we learn the precise
identifications, and holding the engine-revs
evenly for a run." *Unseen over people's lives,*
I thought. "We target Cincinnati, Chicago,
Cheyenne, Abilene. Or Wilmington, Manteo."
"I hear one crashed and buried its nuke
ten miles from my home, beside Contentnea Creek,"
I said. "You will always have the freak accident.
We do everything we can, to prevent
any actual release." "What if one goes off?"
"That can't happen. One would be enough
to wipe away your county from the earth."
"What's it like to fly one?" "It's tough.
Like driving a big truck. The Buff

holds steady, but feels heavy on the controls."
As you pass above houses and schools,
I thought. He had shown me his wife and kid,
their house and wide TV—that they lived as everyone did.
They drove the skies at work, truckers
hauling cargo for a world-ending war.
"What does the acronym stand for?"
"For us, they're big ugly fat fuckers."
I looked around the base. At a far pine wood,
the end of the runway pointed its road
to nowhere. Through the August heat, a waver
distorted the far concrete. I felt space roar
into a vacuum, dissolving the place where I stood.
Then a wind bore a blue smoke from across
the highway, where they barbecued pigs with wood.
I left the base, feeling empty and afraid.
I paid as if with part of my life for a gloss
of grease in the air, haloing my plate
of succulent gray meat. It bit my palate
with a peppery vinegar. Hearing a Buff
take off in a whoosh, I felt myself stuff
down this version of the fallen pig-flesh.
It puts off corruption in a flash,
I thought—*and turns into ash.*

Yet, as I ate, I felt a long-ago
comfort in taste, as the plane for Chicago
or Denver or Kansas City passed over
in that familiar evening, with a nuclear cargo.
As the rushing vacuum absorbed me, my hand
took out the N.C. roadmap—now strange,
as if it charted some foreign land.
I spotted my targeted village, not far down range.

REPAIRING THE FARMHOUSE

Connecting the family graveyard, once,
with the family farmhouse, I faced a gulf
of time and loss, that only a thought could carry.
I felt my ancestral body pause at the highway—
stiff in whispering blades of the head-high corn—
admiring the white straight marks of the upper
and lower porches' railings. The pavement
held me back, like a boundary in Dante.
With no dead poet beside me, I rushed across—
seeing the cars either way, small in their distance.

The oaks in front of the house stood broken-topped
from storms—the chimneys at either end rising man-
tall above the second-floor roof, but missing
bricks in the ornamental finish. Tenants had
lived in it, and been abusive or merely careless
with its legacy, for half the life of my grandfather.
Now, after my father's death, I was having
the tall-paned windows on the further, ground-
floor room restored. With siding re-nailed,
recaulked, with scraping and painting, money had flowed
into this arthritic, stout-beamed structure
like water soaking into dry ground. The set-apart
kitchen had leaked, used as a store-room,
after housing chickens. The peg-joined frame
of the main house held stoutly, indifferent to storms,
its siding mostly original. In the new panes,
with fresh paper stickers, I had missed the ripples
of the other, hand-blown glass. I climbed
the board steps, crossing the eroded porch, and entered
the main room. The view outside, through those window-
panes flawed from the past, distorted the corn-blades
and momentarily magnified a hawk, turning tight discs,

climbing, above the woods-line of Toisnot Swamp.
The walls inside, inscribed by water stains and
illegible countries and landscapes of peeled-
away wallpaper, puzzled me, like erased
blackboards, around a kid who'd missed the class.
I imagined those masters, who had built this ship
to sail across years, on the waves of furrows:
those plowed up and subsiding twice a year,
in the ocean of fields. I sighted the graveyard-
rectangle through a pane of rippled glass, thinking,
that glass is a solid fluid, flowing through centuries.
These panes had hardly had time to sink down thicker
toward the lower edge, as in English cathedrals.
I can inherit this place but not know it,
I thought, going out into the front porch shadow
from which the far headstones of my great-grandfather
and his brother and two wives glowed gray-white
like the time-soiled tallow of candles in sun.
I saw the sweet gum trees over Charlie Sutton's
house in the corner that my father had sold him,
to keep him as mechanic in our garage. Those
starry, lopsided leaves reflected on
a farm pond, its surface inverting
the trees, suspending the current
of the stream which fed it:
as if history were only a picture.

THE HOME PLACE

Heat glazes the trees;
field hands sprung from the land
stand as a darker frieze
where the rows scribe tobacco for miles.
Beyond, forests follow the river's course.
Mules pull the handled wood,
white cotton lines bind
their jaws and necks to the command
of the black man in boots and denim.
Lines in his face remind
of those in this land and in the barn,
behind, near a white house
that preserves an accord in leaves.
There, sun glints the plane
of roof with permanent light. Time
freezes a Somerset precedent, a tinct
smoke-thickening toward evening,
when swallows carve their scrolling
into vapor, like the aura around hair
of the woman who dresses whitely,
fair as this picture in its human
chiaroscuro. The silver the black maid
assembles is English, she speaks half-afraid
across a polished walnut as wide as the Atlantic.
She is illiterate.

Outside, the evening gathers,
illustrious in a scenic vapor
that flavors crevices of these different
oaks with its tannic bitterness.
Distance has exhaled a serene orient
shine into the westward horizon,
as if celebrating illusions layered in glazes

across this landscape: this new place
viewed through flaws in home-
blown panes, by slaves made archaic.
The sweat from dark bodies in fields
for miles condenses in a graciousness.
Tiny motes congregate, gnats
weave over trees as breezes
stir and solidify, in a dense light
where time stops, gelled clear by heat
and bent into an imprisonment.
Along these rows like graves,
the field hands move but lose
their faces into the darkening,
the gathering of miasma from the swamp-
branch behind them, as they troop
cabinward, where already honeysuckle
brushes their bitter breaths with its fragrance.
Time frames this scene for the museum
of the future, to stand
as ideal in the heart of this land.

REFORESTED LAND

Wrought-iron cedars
half-shadowed in woodland edges
scrub the February wind.
The remote cleanliness
of vanished clapboard houses
haunts overgrown clearings—
in some, the fronds of farmyard
jonquils with a few yellow bells
among leaves and briars still
spill their scent where
no one is left to breathe it.
Memory tastes it
across this distance,
this difference of century.
A presence. A wasted fragrance.

A HOTEL TOWER ABOVE OAHU

While blue-black transparent night
floods into Waikiki, street lights
along the Maunalani Heights
come on. Here on the balcony I see
the dingy neighborhoods toward Pearl Harbor
we drove this afternoon. They shine afar
with strung bulbs, and fainter rosaries
of light bead farthest mountains.

Below by the harbor, we walked before sunset.
Within those dimly sparkled arms of land
a few breakers whiten. Yesterday
we saw the bay where Burt and Deborah lay.
You vowed your love, from here to eternity . . .
only, from the long line of spray, I hear
a roar of beginning, of armies clashing.
By our own made lights, we watch
creation spill its accidental beauty.
These necklace-linking bulbs shine back
like galaxies from the dark of Earth
beside the ancient crater of Diamond Head.
The other way, an old war's at anchor
Arizona submerged, leaking oil up toward the stars.

THE LATE APRIL GARDEN

The irises and hydrangeas
as I walk aside abide
in their season. Mallards
congregate on shadowed grass;
they file out, all seven,
young fathers, fatherless
as if to inspect the dust path
they will tread, purposeless
after mating.
I turn with them, aware
of separations, though this air
diffuses the light
around edges of dark and bright.
The hydrangea's pink puff-
surfaces hold spherical stuff
for sight, serving to ignite
the firing of my ganglia.
So existence issues
from an energy-burst, so tissues
support this seeing inside
a *me,* who knows of dead
as well as of living—feels small
and alive, humbled by this wide
brightness which equally for all
spreads the visible enigma
time, in its impermanence.
The silhouette of a pine limb
on the coming evening
refuses to succumb
to the wide Earth's turning.
Pines stand angled, one
plumb straight, *being*
itself, and in reflection

ripple-layered on the pond.
Its distant brokenness in wind
fractures the imaged
boughs, pauses, restores them
in this moment re-imagined.
It fills my breath with its whim
this air of shining in mind.
Each waver of pine tree bright
on the water feels a part
of me, while reflections let
my mind and the world interact.
Then, wind-shattered as I can't predict
the wet reunites with what I am not—
though thought keeps a mirrored light.

CONVERSATION IN FACULTY COMMONS

for Berndt Mueller

He is slender, intellectual, his accent
Austrian—a cosmic theorist.
I studied physics formerly,
loved astronomy as a boy.
Among faculty colleagues,
we talk across salads, in words like these:

"So you think the first universe
primordial—violent—unconscious?"

"Yes," I answer. "Polyphemus,
in the painting by Turner."

"Oh," he says. "The giant that Odysseus blinded.
Then unwisely derided.
But why this cosmos without sight?"

"Because—" I pause. "Withholding light.
Dark at first. Don't you recall
describing to me the first fireball?"

"Yes, I remember. It was the first
time we met."

"You made me imagine the initial zero.
The nothing. The empty O."

"Yes." He pauses. "I recall that
you brightened to hear of the release of light."

"For three hundred and eighty thousand years,"
you told me, "no light appears."

"Yes. But why invoke the Cyclops
at the beginning of the universe?"

"Thinking of origin-unity,
I imagined this being, of only one eye."

"But I thought that we equally sought
descriptions without mythology."

"I start with the earliest instant,"
I say, "in darkness. Then the birth of light."

"So your energy-god—not even a head—
is a blind eyeball instead?"

"My bodiless giant states the paradox:
light in dark, order in violence.
I need to dramatize
the event your numbers realize."

"Very well. Go ahead. Poetize."

"The universe begins as a point.
The first tight sphere of heat
withholds its light,
like an in-turned eyeball
foreseeing all,
and finally evolving sight."

"You mean in the release of light,"
he says. "I accept this poetic mistake.
Early on, the fireball *was* opaque."

"Then it reached a critical boundary,
cooling, and the universe began to see."

"No," he says, sipping coffee. "Not exactly.
The fireball underwent a phase-transition,
reaching a temperature where atoms form.
Then light shone free, this one early time."

"If licensed to be poetical,"
I say, "light is like embodied thought—
beautiful, transiently real.
Physically immaterial."

"Well. Light *is* a materialized energy.
Photons form, in the breaking symmetry.
Light responds, slightly,
to the curvature of gravity."

"Did the freezing of energy, into material form,
create all space and time?"

He considers. "Spacetime arose spontaneously,
with the outward, cooling momentum of energy."

"If matter and energy are one,"
I ask, "inter-convertible, why is the direction
of time one-way—from unity to separation?"

"That is, perhaps, a theological question—
whereon physicists should have no opinion."

"So the universe remains mysterious.
We arise from its violent histories.

Art balances on the precarious
edge."

"Singing of the precipice,"
he says. "You poets are in love with chaos."

"We imagine a different consciousness—
thought-feeling, in a rough embrace."

"Yes," he agrees. "Yet order arose with creation."

"Cosmology supplies a beginning—
an uncanny one, without meaning."

"Physics doesn't deal in opinion.
There is theory, experiment—and verification."

"So unity fell into successive separations."

"We prefer to say, into forces and actions."

"Plotinus speaks of emanations."

"Physics inspires more confidence
than the philosophers of ancient Greece.
Or of Alexandria. However. The emerging
order is richly fostering.
It encodes a tendency
toward coherence, within partial stability."

"The time-world emerges from eternity—
the limited, from infinity."

He frowns, then shrugs. "We
describe such things mathematically—
without auras of divine intent."
He pauses. "Yet there *was* an event,
when spacetime emerged from an a-spatial point."

"I think of it as a first star,"
I say.

        "But containing all others. And far,
far away in time."

        "But how sublime,"
I say.

        "Supremely violent, within exquisite
parameters," he adds.

        "Those elemental constants
that you mentioned once?"

"Yes," he says, "of course. The force
and mass of the universe,
in their almost-perfected balance."

I sigh. "My elementary physics lesson.
Begin with proton and electron."

"Electromagnetic force binds electron
to the nucleus negative to positive."

"So," I say, "and that is how we live."

"Yes," he smiles. "With exactly the energy,
so that atoms interact chemically."

"So that plants, in photosynthesis,
use elemental energy of the cosmos,
once frozen into mass—
now, in its new release,
by the process of solar fusion.
Because of proton and electron."

"You look very pleased with yourself,"
he says, pleasantly. "You simplify
a very great complexity. Such stuff
is part of a feel-good ecology."

"But explain why a universe
exists, rather than nothing. Or chaos."

"The proton and electron, in relative mass.
The strong force, within the nucleus,
in proportion to electromagnetic force.
The lesser, nuclear weak force,
randomly regulating atomic decay."

"Why must there be an instability?"
I ask.

"Atoms unchangeably uniform
would permit no change over time,"
he answers.

"And evolution depends on
variability, between proton and neutron?"

"Eventually. Yes. This partial stability
in the nucleus is held within vaster gravity."

"So the balance of force and mass
allows the stars to coalesce
and burn, in an immense curvature of space?"

"Yes. Shall we have dessert?"
He smiles. "We have order to celebrate."

"Well." I frown. "The star-fields, with gravity,
curve even light into webs of entropy—
within, apparently, dark matter, dark energy."

He sits indecisively. "Perhaps. We don't
quite understand those concepts yet."

"But you believe that you will—
that a clearer theory is inevitable."

"Yes," he says. "That is my belief."

"Entropy is a mortal grief,"
I say. "Time's crooked arrow, pointing one way.
A snake in the garden, as physical decay."

"Well," he says, "all mortality shall not prevent
my enjoying a dessert.
Won't you join me?"

"All right," I sigh, rising heavily.

He chooses blueberry pie, I a chocolate torte.

"Do you find a consolation in taste?"

                                          "Of a sort,"
I say. "But the pleasure is brief."

"Do you need a greater good—some sauce of belief?"

"This time of the cosmos exists without meaning.
It is *beginning,* tending toward *ending.*
Do you see any purpose in the universe?"

"No." He pauses. "Yet it evolved consciousness."

"We are aware, and can know mortality."

He sighs. "Perhaps we miss our childhood religions."

"We live by the meaning in experience,"
I say. "I feel a presence
of the sacred, in the first star
of evening, as light leaks away from the air,
while Earth turns into its shadow."

"You worship within natural wonder,"
he says. "But what *is* the sacred?"

"It is life. Violently born. Endlessly desecrated.
A mysterious value has been seeded
in Earth-things."

                                    "To be appreciated
by a few," he says. "By those like you."

"And yet, science mistrusts the mysterious,"
I say.

                "Theory describes a sublime
universe, within an uncanny spacetime,
as it evolves from initial violence."

"Yes," I reply, "toward the release of light."

"Granted," he replies.

                "I see it in children's eyes,"
I say. "Shining on my granddaughter's corneas,
as she looks out our upstairs windows."

"But the idea of the sacred is dangerous,"
he says. "People kill in its defense.
Imposing it on others, they oppress and mutilate."

"Yet we long for an immaculate light,
while learning not to crucify on mountains,
or sacrifice virgins in volcanoes—
to appease this malicious universe."

"The universe is not malicious,"
he says.

"But violent," I say. "And mindless."

"Not quite," he objects. "Its chaos comprises
these exquisite, uncanny proportions."

"Its order arises,"
I say. "Is its chaotic symmetry an accident?
Is there inevitable metaphor in light?"

"The marvelous relations in nature exceed,
by far, those wonders already described,"
he says. "Present knowledge is a fragment
of the possible."

"Can only the universe hold it?"
I ask.

"Perhaps. But admitting defeat
is a dark way. We collect, age by age,
those fragments which spell out knowledge."

"The time-scale of cosmic origin
exceeds my capacity to imagine,"
I say.

"Perhaps to *feel*, you mean?"

"I *do* feel a melancholy pathos,
for our villages, on shores of the cosmic vastness."

"I understand," he says. "My focus on immensities
relates to the present, subatomic realities.
But at both ends of the cosmic scale,
the objects recede. Spacetime is ineffable."

"Except in its effects," I reflect.
"The little town where I was born
spelled out the sensory alphabet,

with scent of grass, the atmosphere above it,
as fireflies floating on their yellow-green light
made a galaxy of the giant tree—a pecan—
leaf-lacy, cloud-like, a plume for sun
to illuminate, mornings. I ran, my heart
pumping delight. Inhaling vapor, I felt part
of a whole, true son of my region."

"You are fortunate, to have felt your place,"
he says, "in space and time. In the universe."
His eyes look into a distance.
"I belong to this campus. And to CERN."

"Scientists are only human. They behave
as others do. Their theories leave out love."

"Our theories describe what we believe.
They do not prescribe how to live."

"Your work is your religion. Collaborative,
communal—creating your supreme fictions."

He smiles. "I think that phrase Wallace Stevens's."

"Correct. Great maker of language-equations.
Your numbers only outline the skeleton—
which the vividness of life is fleshed upon."

"So you fear that quality
is endangered by scientific quantity?"

"Yes," I say. "Industry and science together
created an iron giant, pure matter.

Its particles seemed wholly determining.
I see it in Victorian engines,
cast iron, vastly lumbering.
The mind can make what it imagines."

"Yet there is a reality outside thought,"
he muses. "Mind and the cosmos interact.
The idea and the fact together fit—
though the theory is only approximate.
No equation is perfectly exact."

"But how can intellect arise from its opposite?"

"Again, a philosopher's conundrum.
The world and its observer correspond.
Matter invites us to wisdom.
Its laws appeal to the mind."

"But whose are these laws? And to what end?"

"The laws emerge, as properties
of original energy—both effect and cause.
The elemental constants arise,
balancing along a knife-edge—
matter slightly exceeding its antimatter opposite.
This first dark heat promised light."

"So my energy-giant
is blindly intelligent?"

"Its burst is our uncanny source—
single, and first. It cools into force
within the atoms' nucleus, into the mass

of proton and neutron. It is visible, as matter."

"Within it are mountains, rivers of water,"
I say.

       "Yes. The desired perfections of form
evolve, within the medium of time.
Piero della Francesca
frescos for us our angel-answer."

"So we dream the universe with our eyes,
and mysteriously, darkly, it replies,"
I say.

       "So it seems."

"Then our purpose is to have better dreams,"
I propose.

       "A quality productive of intelligence
arose with the universe,"
he says. "We are its consequence—
the vivid evidence.
It existed before us."

"But does this evidence imply a purpose?"
I ask.
       "We know the cause by its effects,"
he replies. "We are a consciousness it enacts."

"So we here in our discussion
help to complete creation?"
I ask.

"Yes. If interpreting makes it conscious—
as when experimenters heard a hiss,
and knew it echoed the birth of the universe."

"So the Big Bang is sublime—and sacred,"
I say. "I see it, worshipfully afraid,
and think of Moses on the mountain."

"But the Bell lab listening horn
heard no commandments from God.
It is left us to speak his word.
The echo has cooled—is almost inaudible."

"Do we voice a formative will,
or only a process of chaotic brutalities?"

"Like the randomness in matter,
we uncertainly choose, for worse or better,"
he says.

"Yet humans have moral potential,"
I say. "Mostly, we are merely civil—
or selfishly possessed, by ambitions, or evil."

"My profession seeks the origin of the universe."

"I study and teach the art of verse."

"We value the intellect," he says. "Yet,
like the survivors of a war, we forget
those scenes we cannot face."

"Do you believe in drunkenness?"

I ask.

> "Of what sort—bodily or divine?"

"That from a few glasses of wine."

"Here," he smiles, "they provide only sherry."

"Let's take what is offered, not worry
over ignorance of the sacred mystery."

"Agreed," he says. "Where is the waitress?"

"She comes, like a servant of Dionysus,"
I answer.

> "So. Here's to the light we seek."

"Good," I say. "Let us seek the light—
and trust what evolves from the dark."

The two of us sip wine, are silent.

"And yet," I begin.

> "And yet?"

"The spacetime of galaxies feels radically separate.
Their sublimity is tragic—an icy beauty."

"They organize stupendous creation—
originate worlds, move us with their motion."

"Still," I say, "this is a tragic universe."

"It created time, in which we are conscious."

"Our thoughts of it are fragments—
unconnected dots. Moments, then moments."

"Yet here, together," he says, "we sense
and share an intellectual presence.
Ideas, evoked, exist all at once."

"Perhaps that is the good of the paradigms
of philosophers," I say—"fusing the times
of thought into theorems."

"As a poet makes poems?"
He smiles. Then goes on. "Sometimes,
as I look on a sequence of numbers,
I guess their sense, as one remembers
things past—summers, as scenes of light."

"That is the beauty of things thought,"
I say. "The bright web spun against night."

"But we are, each, the conscious spinner,"
he insists.

        "Yet, in creating, we seem to remember."

"Socrates would say so," he sighs. "We're content
when mentally creating. We forget
things transient."

            "Like coffee and dessert?"

"No," he laughs. "I'll remember the torte
and the pie, when these issues fade into night."

"Time is the tragedy."

            "Only when we recall
our tenuous selves. Envisioning a principle,
the mind feels immortal."

"But only for those moments, when together,
we can so forget—and so remember,
when thought seems recollection."

"Yes. When time is forgotten, in conversation."

"See you again in two weeks?"

"Certainly. Ah, she brings our checks."

FIRST LIGHT

> The Soul thinks in its own way. . . . The One thinks not at all.
> —Plotinus

A beginning uncanny fiat
caught all radiance as in one star—
these beams, like spirit incarnate
encompassing the near and far.

An explosively expanding cosmos
within the dimensionless absolute
condensed its matter from first force
among shafts of immaculate light.

Star-rays, red-shifted, bent—
wave-particles creation has wrought—
shine here from an infinite white
as temporal medium of thought.

The many came from the One,
emanations of a first paradigm—
defining the mind's location
within coordinates of space and time.

THE SHADOWED COUNTERPANE

The penumbra touches my window
the nearer evergreens blacken, the dogwoods,
unlighted, engrave a gray metal horizon.
The platinum-white high air reflects a
pale shine on the bedspread, illuminating lumps
of its tufting as features in a landscape.
It may be a topology of space and time
or a memory of a boy's sickbed
where he lay to recall and imagine—
a yard inscribed by light and shade
when the grass becomes graphite hatchings,
the swallows ink-cursives, on a tissue
of air so thin, this sickle-moon burns through.
The cries of children at play hang muted
in this paradigm world, their running
and gesturing what he had been
drawn away from, to his books and comics.
The stationary children, like numbers,
pose an insoluble problem of longing,
that his tears have long salted away.
This figured horizon returns, a town
he can now revisit, as a syllable-equation.
The past and the passion of its loss persist.
My father is leveling a lawn with his
hand-pushed mower. The light condenses
so nearly into darkness, the spun-back
grass blades incise their bits into the graying—
a cuneiform written in the tablet of memory,
that I read in the dark with my fingertips.
Love reawakens, as from another lifetime—
a pattern of possibility, always present
that I inhabit again, in spite of distance.

IMAGINING ORIGIN

    I

Under the window frame's sliding shadow
cut by the edges which move
I feel the whiteness of the page
the monk's rage to still
his days among mountains.
As I lie upon the counterpane
thoughts snow in unspeakable need
erasing words toward a geometry
of elemental sequence.
This idea lines from an event
a beginning violently complete
in the Big Bang's heat.
I struggle for a spark
in myself to illuminate
intellect, when all is implied
compressed inside—
before syntax
crosses its distance.
I think a new start
acute, star-bright
as if a first conception of light.
So as I imagine
first light takes shape
from the shape of light in thought.

    II

As I seek a first idea
the memory of a star
pierces down from afar.

Once before time-
separation I was one
with myself and my father
and the field outside felt new
to my feet then bare upon it
as I ran the early dew
with Babs and my brother.
Then when my senses whirled
from spinning on grass
I waited on hands and knees
the one to remain in memories
while the turning windows and trees
centered on me as axis—
making my seeing a nexus
of this world with my soul.
Aware before sickness
I felt this separate whole
as breeze on my face, myself
as a leaf in its revolving life.
The begetting constellated
sky above buds of spirea
encircled my one inner light—
my single first point of view.
Now long after, I remember
this being, star-like and true
to myself and my father.

   III

Transparent transient
like materialized thought
light courses the universe—

a visible splendor whirled
creating within its world.

A galaxy displays
its late red-shifted rays
as centering gravity pulls
the stars into their spirals.

Here as I imagine the plain
is almost featureless, counterpane
of a bed and of a country
suspended at evening. I lie
time's invalid remaking the past—
now only skyline, angles
of barn-tin reflecting
at sundown.

IV

As the universe expands
light from receding stars—
dim, red-shifted, bent—
belatedly appears.
My star-created thought
reflects its starting point
and distantly understands.

Silhouettes, a house and barn
shadowed upon the counterpane
establish place in space and time—
a surface locating my own past
and other times to come.

My life which felt first light
a life ago still lives
within the love which was
and ever is.

TIME IN THE FIRST VILLAGE

With the last hymn ended, I believe the shade
of a cedar across from our house already
lengthens—screening us with green-black needles.
I feel us among townsfolk not yet home from
the service, for the sermon has run long.
Before I can wake into the present, I am
with my father and mother and brother Henry
in one lit block between church and our porch.

As much as we try to hasten, light thickens.
My father with his widow's peak—hair slicked
back from his forehead emphasizing the spectacles—
slows in shadow of the last oak and stops.
Henry in short pants and hair blonde white,
as in the light of a sepia photograph or
of a newspaper clipping folded in a trunk,
pauses halfway out and is caught. Mother
stands behind, with her white arms crossed
over her bosom in the nice cotton frock
looking out. Her pout mouth that first
withheld its smile now slowly eases. I am
not among them. Perhaps she recognizes
me in this future I alone live into,
for our family. They feel no sorrow for
me or themselves or each other, turning
with the town in its time toward
evening, the starlight almost beginning.

They wave farewell to me, the eldest son:
still young, my blonde wife now beside me.
They see us as a couple assemble our children.
A daughter is born, with her tiny infant nails,
the first-fine lashes, part of the others' world.

But in this lineal march, we as a separate
family pass on into circles of seeing, perspectives
of later-born souls, which those behind us
no longer share. Yet in another time-order,
those sunlit Sundays, and storms breathing in
their rain through the front porch screens,
and Christmas with a basket of oranges, still exist.
Each yellow-orange sphere of this mountain
of the world, piled under the sky-curved handle,
remains, a part of the life I knew
and was to know: the days to come intuited,
each in its sphere of sun, as one premonition.

As I write this, I come to myself, alone,
as the intense recollection fades, in only
the present. I see the living and those dead,
whom I knew and so loved, as they recede
into the community, where we first walked
from sunlight to shade, then into light.

For a moment I am with my parents and brother
one Sunday, passing through shadow of the willow oaks
and into a permanent sun, on and on, along the block
of sidewalk between the Methodist church and our home.
Unseen, I pass with my family into the house,
where they live and breathe and could not believe
themselves present only in words, safer in history.
The front porch waits, the swing and chairs, where
we may sit to contemplate the evening sky
while it darkens, seeing the curved-wing swallows,
their hieroglyphic arcs expanding as circles,
interconnecting, individuals lost into designs,
as the sharp constellations proclaim a higher order.

MEMBRANE THEORY

Theorists describe spacetime as a mathematical surface, comprising all dimensions in a single topology. I think of this, walking by the Eno, as wave-lines and arcs of rippling weave in uncountable crossings, between the near screen of briars and the opposite shore. The current pulses beside me, its intersecting patterns translucent, like grape pulp. Then again I unfold more of the path through my eyes into memory, subliminally aware of the sensation of effort, as associations flow in an undertone of feeling.

As I add new scenes to this topography, I see a slender, nerve-silver water that threads above bottom-land pebbles, in this riverside, much-folded cortex of earth. The terrain holds paths like a roadmap, connecting me with streets in Durham and Raleigh and Dunn and Kenly, and those spinning out, into ways in Vienna, or Rome. My time and space hold cobblestone impressions, the sedimented Tiber under the Bridge of Angels associating with the Eno's high water. So love is connecting with another, in those other spaces, like learning a foreign country, which is humanly the same, though part of a differently shaped continent. My wife and I felt young again in Rome.

Thinking so, I have wound the path, up from the river and on through the pine wood, where later the owls will call, where sometimes the pileated woodpecker knocks and squawks. Farther, one name-chiseled headstone marks the site of other, found-stone graves—some sunken-in, man-long, or shorter—some, the sizes of infants. Near the chimney-pile of a vanished cabin, jonquils in green-finger fronds try the February wind.

QUEST FOR BEGINNING

The cold front chills me, so I believe
this rumor of pines in wind, distancing
the thought of beginning—and of the star-
simulacrum I will see, if evening
enlightens my path but dims the sky.
Nearer the river, I walk through
a rain of color. Too bright yet
for a sharp-tipped light. I wait
beside sliding water, as the beech grove
uses up day with its yellow.

Not much longer. Wind moans
the limb-vaulted ceiling
like cathedral-conversation with the dead.
Now. Now that this day is fading, clouds
part. A beech ignites like a lantern-mantle.
Is it glow from below,
or one stray ray, descending?

Light leaks away from near air. Higher,
atmosphere catches the sunlight.
When enough of the thickening brightness
passes, I'll see through a clearer night—
and mark the point, infinitely acute,
like the spacetime start.

FIRST STAR

The ridge I climb
slopes up, toward time
for a first star.
I hike where leaf-stuff
left by October covers
this gravity mass I
ride on, whirling. I feel
this pull of the world as it
turns into its shadow.
Atmosphere prisms
the spectrum
of Earth's near star
into a color now thinning where
another will appear.
Careful of foot
I stride the igneous surface
where upthrusts pierce the crust
above the pulse
of Seven Mile Creek.

It is late when I start
back home. I cross
the abandoned clearing
the dense light dimming.
Atmosphere has lost
the brightness that blinds
against transparence.

And there I see it:
this thin end of rays—
one beam twinkling
fragile in its air-lens:

the sharp white
of Vega, like creation's light
regathered in my glance
to a point.

COMING HOME IN THE DARK

I step into shadowing leaves
along corridors in trees
that precede me like a future.
Their parallels open from a point
I project before, conscious
of a behind-me converging into murk.
As the planet rotates its rocky body
it darkens this side with its shadow
leaving the air transparent.
Orion rises, climbing
the sky, seeding space with his stars
begetting new glints in the nebula-sword.

He bequeaths the constellation *demos*
to generations after. I imagine
a marble temple, the metamorphosis
of these trees—trunks now fluted
as a pediment arises among limbs
and a Zodiac begins to pierce through.

Colonnades recede along beams
out-shined from his mind's forms.
Among the great kites of light
Orion's thought shines straight
between the sharp bright starting-points.

With gathering murk at my back
I distill his paradigms
in thought to hold upright
as I descend the path at last
our stream-side house still dark.

Again I look up at the night.
The hemisphere's illusory motion
elevates new arcs into the sky
and I rise with the star-man.

THE LANGUAGE OF SPACE AND TIME

I

The counterpane now is only space—an extent
in light. Once, it encoded a town and belief,
when grass spread wide its uttering tongues
below children. A skyline on the western horizon
seemed cut out of paper. Huge heads of oaks,
those elders, nodded over the low roof-angles
and the wooden bodies below, alive with shouts
and groans, the hopes and mournings. The attics,
seen from inside, held rafters devoutly skyward,
like *Hands in Prayer*. Atmospheres spoke over
these humid lawns, echoing cries between
houses at evening—lightning bugs winking,
enlarging separation, gathering in darkness—
while cooking, that the children smelled from outside
the yellowing windows, bound their tastes to this earth
with more gravity—submerged them in feeling,
their words soft-edged, blurring the consonants,
inflecting bedtime whispers with a particular belonging.
So that Earth may speak of space, it has brewed
these rounded-off, gut-urged surges of breath,
with tastes of long-cooked meat, night in the nostrils.

II

Over the town now shadowed on the counterpane,
lightning flashes. As the storm gathers in upon
the hurried inhabitants, rain in stringent lines
splashes their faces, like the slight weight of rays
from far stars. They look up, and back, tears
of recognition streaming from their eyes.

They have come so far, materialized on this stage
that is the same for everyone, and different.

This possible surface lifts from the Earth
and recedes into time. I behold it departing
with a rending like the soul tearing loose
from my body. And in that moment
I am consoled: by knowing what love is possible,
how so much expands with the new-born light,
in morning, and how this whiteness deepens,
rich with a thousand kisses, shadowed by
this land with its snake-stealthy river,
the air passing under a bridge, enlarged
within the arms and breasts of a lover, along the lone
road at nightfall, in moth-lifting evening.

This remembered fabric, like a counterpane
folded and re-folded between a mother and daughter,
is the membrane of space and time—
surface of love, experience of place
on Earth—a town, somewhere to exist again.

DRIVING FROM COLUMBIA

I

A concrete-block warehouse on
the red-clay sandy edge of town can
occupy the mind—no other sight

so real for miles, only pine barren
land, room for an unnamed longing
when the eye like a brushing hand

moves over the broom sedge field
collecting the down-bowed heads
which uncurl like fern, when the given

wind pressure ceases. Then
sole stalks uplifting one by one
return to sun, reborn. No other

mirror reminds me like pure field
with pine horizon, where I bent to aunts
like saints, the rosiness of broom sedge

all the touch I knew of flesh
arching back to the rustles from heaven.
Desire pools still in horizons, air

held by rain-sheen in gullies;
then the meager lonely country, a tin-
shine half-blinded by bushes,

a mule's shadow burned into
its stall, sky bleak with light
over hay of a different century.

The glazed faces of houses, wood-
crossed panes behind the screens,
with swings on chains, now flash

back the dark car we are to them.
Sunday school's faint call upholds
the steeples, a stick-figure, crucifix life.

The soul, uninstructed, innocent
as a waterfall, iceberg whole,
transparent like broken glass

shatters into needles of desire,
impaling my inner eye
on rays of the sun's thorn crown.

II

Radiant and whole and unknowable,
this interface with fields, that time
spreads out, feels real and unreal,

a material world: space for years
to cross, as I trace the twists and turns
with miles behind us. This present

I disbelieve intersects a wild turkey's
crow-black sheen across the road,
as my fate winds its skein again

from home terrain. I find it still
a glass half-silvered, like soul
under soil, semi-transparent. My love

rides beside, as my hands guide us
over swale and hollow and river,
the houses already dreaming

of lamps at evening. This road-
threaded land, hill-contorted, smoothed
by streams, holds almost our whole life—

as all the ways behind seem
to wind again through time,
as I see in the rear-view mirror—

our story a one of many,
we travelers of the century
we came from. Presently,

I feel us in our last facing
of west turn sundown-golden
in glare through the windshield.

And though of houses left in the past,
behind, some wink out their windows,
others reflect the leveling sun and

prong their shine into the unknown,
blindly lighted, traveling with us.
Our headlights carve the coming dark.

www.ingramcontent.com/pod-product-compliance
Lightning Source LLC
Chambersburg PA
CBHW030123170426
43198CB00009B/718